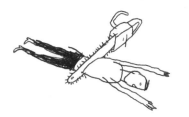

AVOID THIS

Brian Rea

PRINCETON ARCHITECTURAL PRESS · NEW YORK

Introduction

—

When I was about twelve years old, I witnessed a drunk man climb out through the passenger window of a speeding vehicle and up onto its roof. For the next ten miles or so, my family and I—along with the other horrified drivers and passengers on Interstate 495—watched as the man clung to the swerving car like a human clamp. On the spectrum of things not to do, this was way beyond anything I had seen or done up to that point in my life.

In case the significance of this dramatic automotive moment was lost on me and my brothers, my father used it as an opportunity to provide a lesson on how short this "moron's life" would be if he were not lucky enough to make it to the next exit. His sermon and swearing were punctuated by my mother's shrieks and prayers as the offending car veered from lane to lane. It was awesome.

Growing up in a house with three boys, there were plenty of chances to repeat this stunt. In reality, nothing we did came close to it (with the exception of once jumping into a pool from the roof of a house).

To this day, I have never taken a roof ride, but, like all of us, I have been plenty guilty of poor judgment—embarrassing dance moves, various overindulgences, or unfortunate fashion choices. All such episodes can be avoided, but some extend way beyond questionable personal decisions. They can also include uncomfortable situations, surreal circumstances, and, of course, the antics of strange people (awkward, creepy, sinister, or otherwise). The world is a weird place.

Avoid This started as a drawing exercise I did each morning for about a year. I'd wake up and sketch things that made me uncomfortable or laugh—some I observed; others I invented. The idea was always more important than the execution. (There are some bad drawings in this book.) Some sketches are based on my own actions; others express things my friends and family did; and some illustrate news stories or convey the ways of the animal kingdom. I posted the drawings on Instagram—one per day—and the comments ran the gamut from shock (whatever the emoji is for shock) to support (100%, OK sign, etc.). These strong reactions made me think that the audience not only wanted to *see* more, but also needed to see more. It seemed like a collective hope that we all look more closely at what's happening around us.

It should also be said that this book is not a barometer to measure, modify, or correct behavior. I have no recommendations on how anyone should behave. That would be a terrible book. *Avoid This* celebrates what we've already done. In all the awkwardness and glory of these moments, there is charm and humor and anxiety and all the other emotional stuff that makes us human. It is a record of observations and a mirror to all the missteps made or accidents waiting to happen—an ode to our reckless behavior and our wonderful vices.

The episodes and moments drawn in *Avoid This* land everywhere on the spectrum of awareness. Some are almost impossible to notice; others are life-threatening activities (like the man on the roof of the car). But they all share a common theme: human nature. They are us. *Avoid This* is for all of you.

Brian Rea

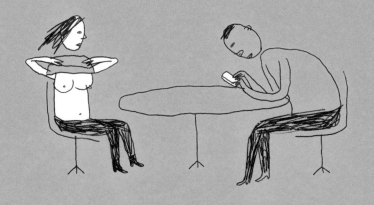

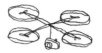

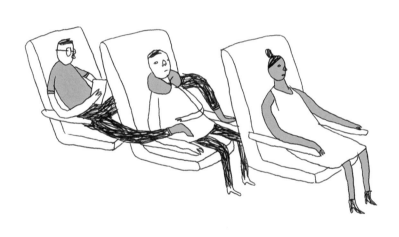

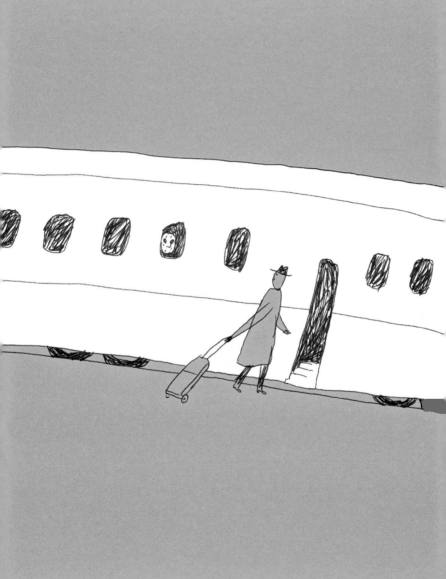

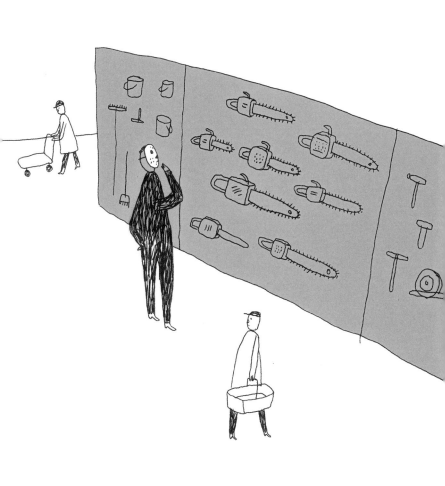

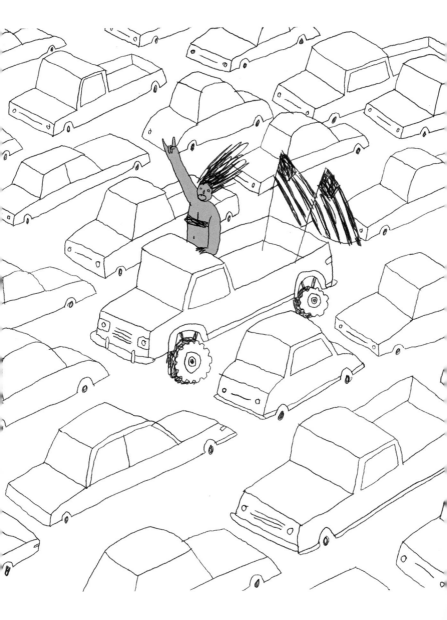

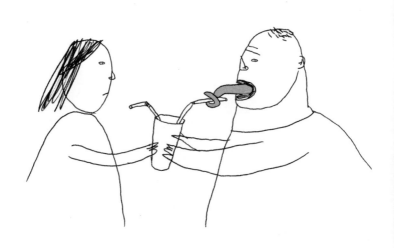

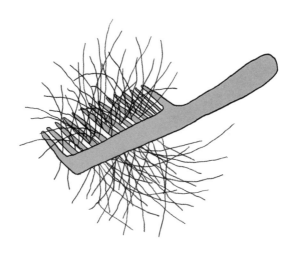

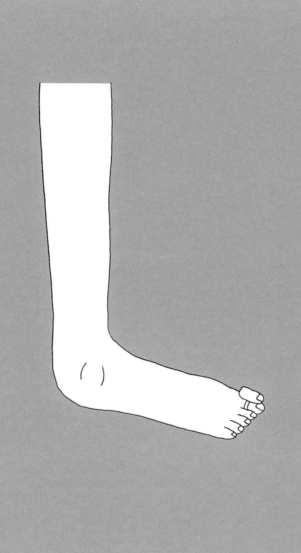

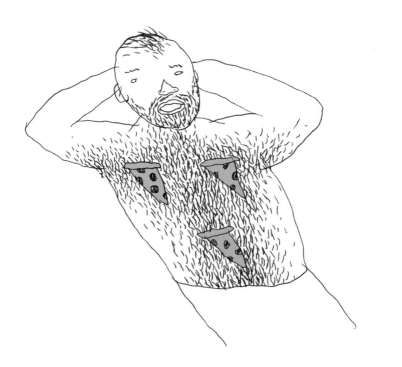

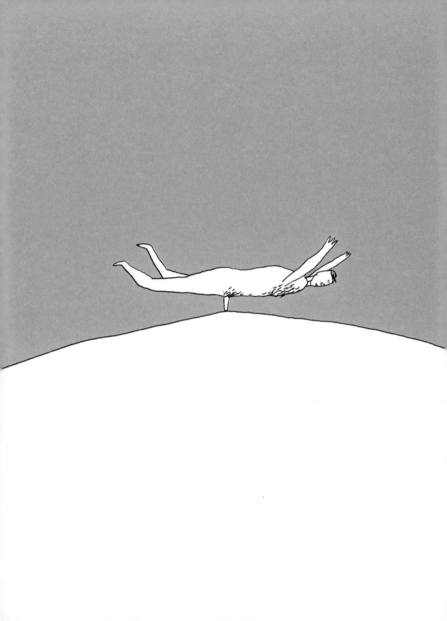

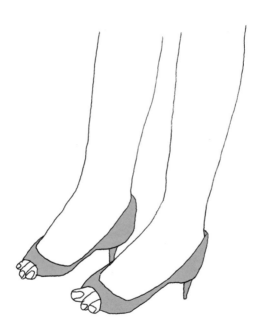

Brian Rea produces drawings and paintings for books, magazines, murals, and fashion and film projects around the world. He is the weekly illustrator for the Modern Love column in the *New York Times*, and he has exhibited work in Paris, Seoul, Los Angeles, Mexico City, and Barcelona at the Fundació Joan Miró. He lives in California with his wife, his son, and his plants.

To Paul and Mike for keeping me out of trouble. Mostly.

PUBLISHED BY
Princeton Architectural Press
202 Warren Street
Hudson, New York 12534
www.papress.com

ISBN 978-1-61689-958-5

EDITOR: Sara McKay
DESIGNERS: Brian Rea, Paul Wagner

Library of Congress Cataloging-in-Publication Data available upon request
Library of Congress Control Number: 2020936028